Mind Training For Martial Artists

Rory Christensen

DEDICATION

To my dog Sandy, my faithful companion for the last ten years.

Contents

Introduction

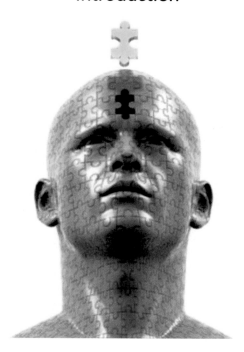

"You will only climb as high as your mind lets you"—**Robyn Erbesfield**

"One man that has a mind and knows it will always beat ten men who haven't and don't."—**George Bernard Shaw**

The training of the mind is something that is often neglected amongst martial artists. It is generally accepted that the martial arts help to develop the mind, body and spirit, yet the mind and spirit are usually forgotten about as we put all our efforts into mastering the more physical techniques within the martial arts.

I believe that training the mind is just as important as training the body, for were the mind goes the body follows, something many of us forget in our pursuit of physical mastery.

It is almost impossible to achieve our full potential as martial artists unless we acknowledge the fact that the mind plays a significant role in our overall development.

It is the key to all growth and without it we are merely puppets on a string, all physical movement and lacking in the depth and understanding that's absolutely necessary to take us to the higher levels of mastery.

Many of us are pretty much in the dark when it comes to actually training the mind. How do you train something that doesn't exist in physical form? Training the body is easy because it exists in physical form. We therefore have something real and substantial to work with, plus we can easily see if we are making progress or not because the body lets us know, in different ways (through better movement, higher skill levels etc.) that we are improving.

Just because the mind is ethereal however, doesn't mean it can't be trained. We simply think of the mind as another muscle that can be worked and developed like any other muscle on our bodies and suddenly it doesn't seem so difficult. The trick now is coming up with ways and methods to actually do this and then properly gauging the results off our efforts.

The mind is so powerful that we can train it do almost anything we want with enough hard work, patience and know-how. That's all it takes. So in that sense we just treat it like we would any other part of our body.

But, you may be asking, *"Why do we need to train our minds for martial arts? I can punch, I can kick, in fact I am bloody brilliant when it comes to technique. How is mind training going to make me any better?"*

Well let's see shall we.

How the Mind Works

So just what is the mind? If we are going to get any use out of the mind, we need a definition that is useful.

Although the word "mind" leads us to believe the mind is a thing, it is not. The mind is a label we have given to an active and dynamic process of thinking, perceiving and experiencing.

The term "mind" refers to a never-ending flow of information processing. The mind is never static. It is a constant stream of sensory in- put, thoughts, ideas and perceptions. It's a continuous dance of information, a ceaseless stream of awareness in which almost anything can be swept up.

Just because we can't see the mind does not mean it cannot be trained. The mind can be trained in much the same way as the body, through diligent practice of the right techniques.

Directing and guiding this awareness is the mind, which we can think of as a system that directs our information processing.

The system of information processing we call "the mind" can also be called our internal reality. We each have an external reality- the environment we live in, the circumstances of our lives - and we each have our own unique internal reality. It is this internal reality that lies behind emotions, behaviour and results.

Our inner reality is far from a random mess of mental chaos. Human subjective experience has a structure. Knowing the specific elements that make up the structure of our internal reality enables us to alter the structure so that it serves us better.

In order to reprogram our minds and upgrade our mental software to produce superior results, we must begin by bringing those hidden programs to the surface. Once we know what is operating in the mind we can run some antivirus software, uninstall outdated programs and upgrade where possible.

Most of us race to have the latest cell phone and the newest gadget, but why do we keep running obsolete mental software?

Don't worry, when you begin to explore your mind you won't find inner demons waiting to be freed or terrible things wanting to bubble up as Freud would have you believe. You will, however, very likely find some old programs that you may no longer want.

Remember, they are just programs and if you installed them, you can uninstall them.

Benefits of Mind Training

So as a martial artist what kind of benefits can you expect to get from training your mind? Well first of all, training the mind in the way that we will be discussing will not only help improve you as a martial artist, it will also help improve you as a person in other areas of your life, in much the same way as your existing martial arts training has probably improved your life so far.

By training in martial arts you have already been training your mind whether you know it or not. Training the body is training the mind, and vice versa.

What we are going to try and do, with the use of the techniques and information contained in this book, is to be a little more conscious about training our minds, which means focusing on actually doing so rather than just having our minds trained as a by-product of training our bodies.

Isolating the mind for training will also allow you to focus solely on certain aspects of your martial arts training and thus develop those aspects much more than you probably have been doing up to this point. In effect, you will be taking control of your own mind and using its powers to further develop your abilities as a martial artist.

The benefits to be gained from consciously directing your mind power are almost limitless, limited only in fact, by the amount of time and effort you put into doing so, just like regular martial arts training. The more you put into it, the more you get out of it.

To train the mind it is just a matter of learning some basic principles and techniques which you can then use to improve specific aspects of your training.

The aspects you choose to improve are entirely up to you. You may choose to develop and improve your speed, your power, particular techniques or even your attitude and your way of looking at and dealing with certain situations such as street self defense situations or competitive fights.

At the end of the day, as long as you know the basic principles of mind training you can be as creative as you like with their application.

Now, let's dive straight in to laying the groundwork for mind training and delve into meditation...

Chapter 1: Meditation

"To the mind that is still, the whole universe surrenders." — **Lao-Tzu**

"Meditation brings wisdom; lack of mediation leaves ignorance. Know well what leads you forward and what hold you back, and choose the path that leads to wisdom." — **Buddah**

If we wish to make the mind receptive enough to the training we want to put it through then we first have to lay the groundwork in order for us to do that.

Meditation is the corner stone of our mental and spiritual development and it is the foundation on which all the rest of our mind training exercises are built. It is therefore probably the most important aspect to any kind of mind training regime, for it will enable us to reach those places in our minds that we need to reach in order to affect the changes needed to improve our performance as martial artists.

Mediation is obviously not new in the martial arts and indeed it has functioned as a vital part of martial arts philosophy and development right from the start. To a large degree its practice within the martial arts has made the martial arts themselves a spiritual and mental endeavour that lifts them above mere physical pursuit.

The art in martial arts largely came from the focused and calm minds of habitual mediators, visionaries who were able, through meditation practice, to see beyond mere physical technique and lend the martial arts a depth that very few other physical activities have.

Meditation offers us a way to view our souls and get a sense of what the universe really is.

For anyone who may never have tried mediation for any length of time, what I just said there will sound completely ridiculous. *"How the hell do you see all that by sitting with your eyes closed for a while?"* you may be thinking. *"I lay every night with my eyes closed and all I see are whacked-out dreams!"*

Well, the fact of the matter is that you do see these things, for whatever reason. It's almost a feeling of gradually coming awake and suddenly you can feel and sense and see these things about yourself and the world; things that are very helpful to you as a person. You begin to feel different--more alert, more focused and more conscious.

You become much more capable of doing things. You don't feel so overwhelmed all the time.

You begin to establish a spiritual connection with yourself and the universe that goes above and beyond anything that our made up religions can offer. It's actually meaningful and it constitutes a fully-fledged spiritual awakening.

All of that is perfectly achievable through regular meditation practice and all of it is commonly what most people experience when they seriously commit themselves to it.

Its benefits are more than just understanding and inner experiences; its benefits also affect the real world in which you live and operate, they make you better at the things you do normally in everyday life, including martial arts.

Zen and the Martial Arts

Zen and martial arts share the development of Samadhi: one-pointed concentration (a state of consciousness beyond waking or sleep in which conscious mental activity ceases so to allow total absorption with the object of concentration).

To have deep Samadhi we have to allow all mental disturbances to cease – disturbances including anger, hatred, greed and so on.

Through the practice of regular meditation we are able to keep these mental disturbances under control enough that they don't affect our outlook or performance in life.

As regards martial arts training the practice of Zen or meditation will better enable you to keep the negative emotions like fear and anger out of your practice. Technique should not be fuelled by any particular emotion, especially anger, for it will corrupt the flow of it and lead to stiffness and lack of fluidness in your movements.

Your action in practice ought to be natural and spontaneous. Spontaneity is a word that is closely associated with Zen, and with advanced practice of martial arts. The word was a favourite of Bruce Lee's, but I think it's often misunderstood. People sometimes take it to mean impulse.

In reality, spontaneity is only possible after you get rid of hindrances (such as negative emotions) and become free of the disturbances they cause. Spontaneous action is not a matter of untrained impulse.

Advanced practitioners of the martial arts have assimilated all the technical advice into their bodies and minds, and in a sense are now able to act spontaneously. That's apparent when you see someone who's really good and who appears to move without thinking. They exhibit a great naturalness and that should be the goal of anyone trying to master technique.

Regular meditation practice can improve your martial arts by helping you stay focussed and relaxed. The key is to do it every day to get a cumulative effect.

Zen meditation will greatly help you along the path to naturalness; to spontaneity and fluidness of movement. It will allow you to de-clutter your mind and help you go with the flow of whatever technique you happen to be performing.

As well as these primary benefits, the meditative state also affords you the opportunity to implant new ideas and positive beliefs and emotions into the mind. It then becomes possible to work on changing yourself for the better. This deep connection with the mind is essential to the impact of the exercises that will be introduced in later chapters.

Calming the mind in the way that meditation does, de-cluttering it of disturbances, makes the mind a fertile place for new positive mental growth, which will of course translate into improved martial arts performance.

Just to recap before we move on the meditation exercises: meditation enables one to calm the mind, clear it of mental disturbances and negative emotion and replace them with deep concentration and focus as well as the ability to be spontaneous in training. The advanced mental states achieved also allows one to relax deeply enough so that we may communicate with the subconscious part of the mind and reprogram it to our liking, updating the software found there so that it works with us and not against us.

How to Meditate

Meditation itself is not very difficult to do and with enough practice you will soon get used to any mental or physical discomfort that may occur. Just as in martial arts practice, meditation is a technique that must be practiced and refined in order to get it right and to get the full benefits from it that we have talked about.

Begin by finding somewhere quiet where you won't be disturbed for a while, like a room with no one else in it. It doesn't really matter where you go, as long as it's an environment that is free of visual and auditory distractions, a place where you can sit and be alone with yourself and your mind.

There are no set rules that govern the practice of meditation which means you can alter the practice to suit yourself.

In terms of what position to adopt while actually doing it for instance, you can sit whatever way you wish. I personally like to do it from a kneeling position with the hands placed on top of the thighs, in much the same way as you would kneel in the dojo. I just find this position the most comfortable.

Other people like to adopt the classic Zen position of sitting cross-legged with the hands cupped in the lap. Again, it is down to personal preference. If you wish to sit in a chair and meditate then do so. As long as you adopt a position that allows you to keep you're back fairly straight and your breath flowing easily.

Lying on your back is not something I would recommend you do for your body tends to associate this position with rest and sleep and so you will quickly find yourself becoming too relaxed and you will probably fall asleep, which is not what we want to achieve.

What we want to achieve through meditation is a quiet mindfulness, which means that you will be more or less awake but relaxed enough that you will be able to dispassionately observe the goings on of your mind.

When you have adopted a position that you can sit in for a while, close your eyes and begin to breathe deeply through your nose, taking the breath all the way down into your belly until you feel it expand like a balloon. When the balloon is full, release the breath through the mouth, allowing all the air to leave the belly until empty and then repeat. Do this type of deep breathing about ten times, feeling yourself relax with every breath, allowing any tension or negative emotion to drain from your body and mind.

At this point you can begin to breathe normally again or you can continue to take deep breathes. It's really up to you. I tend to continue with the deep breathing for two reasons. One is that deep breathing in this fashion is very beneficial to your health, exercising the lungs and oxygenating the body. The second reason is that it gives me something to concentrate on so that I'm not dwelling on whatever thoughts happen to cross my mind.

The object of meditation at this point is simply to sit quietly and allow whatever thoughts happen to pop into your head (and there will be a deluge, especially at the beginning of your practice) to simply pass by.

Many people think that you have to somehow empty your mind of thought, but this is an impossible task. Instead you simply don't engage with your thoughts. You just acknowledge them for what they are and let them pass across the window of your mind.

You will most likely have difficulty at first in not engaging with your thoughts and you may even find yourself being drawn deeply into them for a time. If you find this to be the case all you have to do is simply shift your attention once again back to your breathing. Each time you feel your concentration shift, just bring yourself gently back to your breathing and don't give yourself a hard time for loosing concentration.

Remember, the point of meditation is to release yourself from negative emotion, not further add to it by being critical of yourself. Give yourself a break.

Start your sessions of by staying in meditation for about ten to fifteen minutes at a time, twice a day, maybe once in the morning and once at night. I find this length of time sufficient to get the full benefits from the practice. As you get more advanced you can increase the amount of time you stay in the meditative state. Some people spend an hour at a time in it, it's up to you.

One thing I will say is that you shouldn't allow yourself to get too caught up in meditating. At the end of the day it is just a tool to help us along in life and you should spend most of your time engaging with reality as opposed to hours on end engaging with the wonders inside your head.

Meditation is an art in itself and what I have given you here is just the basics to get you started. If you want to take things further then I suggest you check out the resources listed at the end of this book.

Moving Meditation and the Martial Arts

Meditation can be practiced anywhere. It does not always involve sitting in a static position. It is possible to meditate while walking or running or doing any other activity such as martial arts.

At the end of the day meditation is about cultivating mindfulness and you don't have to be sitting still to achieve this.

Indeed one of the best forms of meditation I have found is kata practice. The practice of kata requires one to be in that mindful state of awareness were we are totally in the moment, focused only on the movements of the kata and nothing else. The movements actually help one to dampen down the mental disturbances we talked about earlier so that we can reach that state of Samadhi, of ultimate concentration.

Zanchen kata is actually designed with this purpose in mind. The movements, done very slowly and deliberately, are perfectly synchronised with deep breathing, allowing one to fall into that state of complete focus and concentration until all else is blocked out of the mind. Mind and body are working in perfect harmony.

If the intention is there then you can bring this state of mindfulness to all of your training, were nothing comes between you and the technique you are performing. The mind and body are effectively performing in unison, focused on the singular goal of a correct and unified performance of whatever technique you happen to be doing.

This translates into true Zen in the martial arts.

Mokso

Let me just end this chapter by mentioning the practice of *Mokso*, something many of you will be aware of already, especially the traditionalists amongst you. *Mokso* is something I've been doing ever since I started in the martial arts years ago.

Mokso is basically the act of remaining still, both inside and out. Very much like meditation it involves kneeling down and concentrating only on your breathing, once again allowing your thoughts to pass you by unhindered.

Done at the beginning of class, Mokso allows you to get yourself calm and focused for the training ahead, giving you the mindfulness we talked about earlier.

Done at the end of class, Mokso allows you re-centre yourself and calm the mind and body after vigorous physical training so that you leave the dojo, not hyped up, but in a harmonious state.

If you don't already practice Mokso in the dojo then I suggest you give it a try and see what a difference it can make to your mental state and your overall training.

Now let's take a look at some of the techniques we can use to improve ourselves while actually in that calm and relaxed state, starting with the cinema of the mind...

Chapter 2: Visualization

"When confronted by a situation that appears fragmented, step back, close your eyes and envision perfection where you saw brokenness. Go to the inner place where there is no problem and abide in the consciousness of well- being." --**Alan Cohen**

"I train myself mentally with visualization. The morning of a tournament, be- fore I put my feet on the floor, I visualize myself making perfect runs with emphasis on technique, all the way through to what my personal best is in practice…. The more you work with this type of visualization, especially when you do it on a day-to-day basis, you'll actually begin to feel your muscles contracting at the appropriate times." --**Camille Duvall**

In the last chapter we looked at meditation and its usefulness in opening up our consciousness and creating fertile ground for the changes we want to make to take root.

In this chapter we are going to look at an underrated technique that when done correctly can be very powerful and very effective in aiding our development, not only as martial artists but also as people in general and that technique is visualization.

What is Visualization?

Visualization (or creative visualization as it is sometimes known) is the act of creating visual images in your mind for the benefit of changing future behaviour.

The idea is that if you wish to change some aspect of your behaviour or personality then you conjure up an image in your mind that depicts you actually behaving in the way that you wish to behave. You do this often enough over time and you will affect real changes.

Or to put it another way, we change our external reality by changing our internal reality.

The reason visualization works so well is because your mind communicates with your body through images. The brain processes "imagined" and "real" events in very similar ways. The same visual centres of the brain are stimulated, for instance, when you see something in the dark and when you imagine it. And because information in the brain is stored, not in isolation but in association, visual stimuli trigger emotional, sensorial, mental and physiological responses.

If, for example, you happen to have a wound on your hand, you can't talk to it and tell it to heal itself because it just won't. If however, you picture the wound on your hand shrinking and healing then many studies have shown that it will heal significantly faster.

One theory for this is that your mind is afraid of unknowns and considers them to be "pain", while it considers "knowns" to be pleasure, regardless of how unpleasant they may actually be. This means that once you have put that image into the "knowns" category in your head, your brain will stop fighting against you and will do everything possible to make it happen. This can work for either physical or emotional challenges.

An emotional challenge may be anxiety before a grading, fear of confrontation or apprehension before a competition fight. Once you can visualize the association of calmness or excitement to be connected to being graded or confronted in a fight, you will physically begin to feel different in that situation. By appropriately using visualization to associate positive emotions and outcomes with these situations, your feelings of anxiety, fear or apprehension will fade away.

So when done correctly, visualizing yourself doing something can actually be just as effective as actually doing it.

Further proof of this has been documented in a study made some years ago involving two groups of people who were asked to throw a basketball through a hoop. One group was asked to practice visualizing themselves shooting the hoops in conjunction with physical practice, while the other group was asked to do nothing but physical practice. Guess which group had the higher success rate in the final test? That's right, the group who visualized beforehand. They beat the other group by a significant margin.

So we have well established that visualization actually works and that it can have a significant impact on performance, so let's now look at how to actually do it in practice.

How to Visualize

To get the most out of visualization you must first put yourself into a suitably relaxed state so that your mind will be susceptible enough to the images you wish to show it. So just like in the meditation practice find yourself a quiet room to be in for at least fifteen minutes or so and make sure it is free from all distractions.

There are no hard and fast rules as to how you put yourself into the required relaxed state. You can make visualization a part of your meditation sessions by simply doing it when you have finished your deep breathing, as I tend to do, or you can alternatively sit in a comfortable chair or lie down on a bed and progressively relax your body and mind, which works equally well.

Lying down a bed is a good way to get yourself really relaxed but again, like I mentioned in the last chapter, you have to be careful you don't end up falling asleep. I have laid down on my bed visualising many times before, and it's fine as long as you stay conscious enough and concentrate on the images you're creating. Whatever works for you is fine.

When it comes to visualisation, the more relaxed you are the better. You want to get yourself down into an alpha wave brain state, which is the most relaxed you can get without actually falling asleep.

In this particular state of consciousness you will have a better connection with your subconscious mind. Going into deep relaxation is like opening up a communication port between your conscious and unconscious minds, making it easier to pass information – in this case images- between the two.

There are a number of different ways to put yourself into this state, but one method that I have found to be particularly effective is using a hypnosis video that I found on YouTube about a year ago. I was preparing myself for an upcoming kickboxing match when I came across this and I found using it to be a quick and easy way of putting myself into the desired alpha state. If you're like me then you don't have a lot of time to devote to these sessions, so finding something like this was a real God-send for me.

All you have to do is slip on some headphones and follow the instructions given in the video. When you get to the part near the end where the voice asks you to step through the door into your unconscious, just pause it at that point and then begin to do your visualization. Once you've finished, hit play and the voice will bring you back around to full wakefulness again.

Here's the video. Check it out.

https://www.youtube.com/watch?v=lNHa_0cgWUc

So before we actually look at how visualisation can improve your martial arts, let run through a few general pointers that you should keep in mind when visualising:

When visualizing, it's important to view the action from the first person — that is, see yourself achieving your goal (i.e. the behaviour you want to change or improve) through your own eyes, rather than watching yourself from the outside. This method is very powerful because this is the way you already see and experience everything. Less powerful is viewing your goal from the third-person perspective, seeing yourself achieving the goal as if you were watching a movie. It still works, but it's not as effective as viewing from the first-person perspective.

Make visualization fun. You will have more success with the technique if you picture yourself actually enjoying whatever it is you're doing. This seems to take away some of the stress that comes from the need to perform correctly. You put enough pressure on yourself in the real world without perpetuating and adding to it in your visualizations as well. So have fun with it as much as possible.

When you're visualizing try not to project into the future, but instead see yourself as if you are doing things now, right this minute. Seeing yourself doing things in some distant future is signalling to your brain that your goal will always be of in the future and therefore constantly out of your grasp. See yourself achieving now and you're more likely to find success for your mind will be tricked into thinking your goal has already been achieved.

The more real your image is, the better. Make the image not just a still picture, but a full-length movie starring you. Replay it over and over, seeing yourself as the hero, achieving your goal. Create background music, pump it up, make it feel real, and have fun with it. This is how you want to see your goal — in vibrant Technicolor on an IMAX screen — not in dim, dreary, out-of-focus scenes shown on a shoebox-size theatre in the multiplex of your mind.

Visualization for Improved Martial Arts

To improve yourself as a martial artist through visualisation it is just a matter of deciding what you want to be better at and then visualizing yourself doing better by following the guidelines above.

As an example, if you wish to improve a particular kata, then you would first get yourself into the required alpha state (deep relaxation) and then you would picture yourself in your mind performing that kata as near perfectly as you can imagine, all the while enjoying the whole process. You will be basically creating in your mind a full colour movie, and the star of that movie will be you. You will be aware of every sight, sound, smell and feeling as you do this. You will be aware of the positive emotions associated with practicing the kata. Your goal is to make things as real as possible so your mind is tricked into thinking that what is happening is reality.

Many people also only use one out the possible five senses when visualizing (sight) which tends to lessen the effect of the exercise, which is why psychologists often say that it is much better to use the three out of five rule, which basically means using three out of your five senses to heighten the effect of the exercise.

Tom Platz, one of the world's greatest bodybuilders has also been quoted thus:

"If you can use five of your senses in visualization practice I'm confident that you can triple the results of your visualization process."

You do this regularly, every day if possible, for ten to fifteen minutes at a time until you feel reality has caught up with your imagination. It's really up to you when you want to stop. It just depends on how well you wish to improve.

Marked improvement can usually be achieved after a few days of visualizing but for best results it is advisable to keep at it for longer. Real improvements can take anywhere from be- tween twenty and thirty days, so a certain amount of diligent practice and patience is required if you want to make real gains in your progress.

Visualisation can be used for anything. You can use it to improve your speed, your flexibility, your power, certain techniques; it can be used to help you prepare for a competition, to dampen anxiety (just picture yourself being calm and collected) or even to be a better teacher. The possibilities are endless and are limited only by your needs and the depth of your imagination.

Geoff Thompson, one of the world's most renowned martial artists and famous for his books about his nightclub bouncing days, has said that he often practiced visualization before he went out to work as a doorman in the nightclubs. In that sense, he found its practice an invaluable asset.

If you need further proof of this techniques validity then try this. Go into the side splits, spreading your legs as far out as you can. Are you at full stretch? Good, now close your eyes and imagine yourself going even deeper into the stretch, really picture it in your mind, feeling the burn in your legs. Now open your eyes and try to go even further into the stretch. I guarantee you will be able to go down further than you did the first time. I also guarantee that if you do the exercise again you will get even further again. Try it!

Visualization for Street Self Defense

Visualisation for self defense is a bit of a double-edged sword. On the one hand visualizing yourself competently handling a self defense situation will help you greatly if you happen to find yourself in one in real life. On the other hand, vividly imagining yourself in such situations brings with it the danger of actually drawing them to you through the very real and very powerful law of attraction.

To imagine a situation in great detail and to do so emotively and on a regular basis will put out there in the universe that you actually want this situation to happen. The danger is you could be walking down the street some day and you will suddenly find yourself in the very situation that you have been so vividly imagining in your head! In that case, you'd better make sure that you pictured yourself handling that situation very well or you're in trouble. So just be aware of that when you decide to imagine yourself being attacked.

If you don't have a lot of confidence in your ability to handle a street attack then visualization is one way to help you gain more confidence in that area. All you do is create a situation in your mind were someone is attacking you and you then see yourself reacting to that attack with full skill and confidence.

If you imagine the situation well enough then you should be able to feel the adrenaline and the fear coursing through you as if it was actually happening. Just see yourself coping with all that and doing what you have to do to manage the situation, whatever that may be.

Visualizing in this way is very effective for getting you used to the flood of feelings and emotions that come with street attacks. It's a way to experience the extreme pressure of it all without actually being there in reality, although as far as your mind is concerned, you are there.

Chapter 3: Focus

"Get out of the blocks, run your race, stay relaxed. If you run your race, you'll win. Channel your energy. Focus." –**Carol Lewis**

"Our thoughts create our reality– were we put our focus is the direction we tend to go." –**Peter McWilliams**

"Goals provide the energy source that powers our lives. One of the best ways we can get the most from that energy is to focus it. That is what goals can do for us; concentrate our energy." –**Denis Waitley**

Success in any activity is in large part due to how well you can focus your mind to bring about that success. In the two previous chapters we have looked at meditation and visualization, both of which are practices that essentially focus the mind in a certain direction. In this chapter we are going to look at how we can focus our minds even further for martial arts success, both in the long term and in the immediate, short term. So let's begin by looking at what it means to focus the mind.

What is Focus?

Put simply, to focus the mind is to put all of your attention on a singular goal or activity to the exclusion of all else. In martial arts terms, if we wanted to achieve focus in training then we would concentrate all our attention on whatever technique we happened to be doing at any given time. So if you're practicing a throwing technique then you're practicing a throwing technique, you're not watching someone else out of the corner of your eye, having a conversation or thinking about what you should do later, even though this is what a lot of people do in training. By not focusing you are slowing down your progress.

For most martial artists it is just a matter of turning up to training, getting the class in and going home again. There is no clear focus as to what they wish to gain from the training, if anything. Many martial artists make the mistake of believing that the class structure set by the instructor is enough to keep them focused, but in the end you are really working to someone else's agenda, not your own.

Let me just say here that I don't have a problem with someone who wishes to just train for the sake of training. There is nothing to say that you can't do something just for the love of doing it. What I am saying here is that if you want to really advance and make steady, measured progress--on your own terms--then you have to have some kind of focus, a well thought-out and clearly defined direction in which you want to go.

The key to having good focus to know exactly what you want to gain from your training and how to go about getting it.

Having a clearly defined sense of focus means you will not be working to someone else's goals and being pulled in the direction that they want you to go in. So really, by having focus, you are taking back control and defining your own path again, which to my mind is what training in the martial arts is all about, self-expression through forging your own path.

To put it another way, if you don't take the time to get really clear about what it is you want to accomplish, both in life and in the martial arts, then you will be forever doomed to spending your time achieving the goals of those who do. And why would you want to do that? Surely that's enough reason to get yourself some focus and define where it is you want to go?

Types of Focus

There are three types of focus that really matter:

1. Overall or Life-Time Focus. To have an overall focus that governs just about everything you do is to have a clearly defined purpose in life, or in our case, the martial arts. All your other goals and all the other things you choose to focus on will be subservient to and geared towards achieving this overall goal.

It is therefore up to you to decide what it is you generally want out of martial arts training. Why are you training? Ultimately what do you wish to gain from all that training?

Working this out requires a bit of time and thought but when you have a clear idea of what it is you want to achieve overall you will find yourself being much more focused and much more secure, both in your training and in your identity as a martial artist.

You will no longer just be a martial artist who trains, you will be a martial artist who trains with a clearly defined sense of purpose and that can make all the difference not just to your progress but to your overall confidence. Knowing exactly why you are standing in that dojo will lend you great focus in itself.

To help you work out what your overall focus should be, try this simple but effective exercise. Take a pen and a piece of paper and write at the top of the page, "What Is My Martial Purpose?" or even, "Why Do I Train?" Spend at least the next twenty minutes writing down whatever comes into your head in response to this question. Don't censor yourself, just let the answers flow until you eventually come up with a deep and meaningful answer that sums up why you train and explains why you keep going back to the dojo. Stick at it for as long as it takes to come up with an answer that is meaningful to you. It doesn't have to mean much to anyone else, just you.

Give the exercise a go and see how you get on. You may be surprised as well as moved by the answer you come up with.

2. Long Term Focus. Having long-term focus means having goals that you want to achieve over a longer period of time. The length of time will depend on the goal you are focusing on. If one of your long-term goals is to get to black belt stage then that could obviously take years to achieve, especially if you have just started in the martial arts.

Another long-term goal might be to win your first competitive fight or to be able to kick at head height. The goals will be as varied and as different as those who set them. The point is that they will take months or years to achieve.

Creating a long term focus through the use of long-term goals will give you something to work towards over time and it will further focus your individual training sessions, for all your training will be geared towards eventually achieving these goals.

The trick to achieving your long-term goals is to break them down into shorter goals that you can work on and achieve in the short-term. Your every training session will then be spent doing something that will bring you closer to achieving your longer range goals.

3. Immediate Focus. Immediate focus equates to being in the moment and having full concentration on what you are doing. You have your goals, you know what you need to do to achieve them, now you must focus entirely on doing that. Later we will discuss how you can better focus yourself in the moment, but for now let's take a look at goals and how to set them.

How to Set Goals Properly

Most of you reading this will at least be aware of the importance of setting goals in life so I'm not going to spend a lot of time trying to convince you of the benefits. All I will say is this. If you go through your life without a clear idea of where you want to go and what you want to be, someday you will find yourself looking back and saying to yourself, *"How the hell did I end up here?"*

As a martial artist you will end up asking yourself the same question after twenty years or more of training if you don't define what it is you want to achieve in your training.

If you had an idea that you wanted to learn self defense and you joined a very traditional karate class then you are going to be sorely disappointed after so many years of training when all you can do is kata and strike from a low stance. You would have been better choosing a style more geared towards self defense in the beginning. If you had had goals and a sense of direction your choices would have been better. You may have left after a few sessions and went to another club where you could better achieve your goals.

Some people also make the mistake of thinking that because they have a direction, they must therefore have goals, but this is not the case and merely creates the illusion of progress. A goal is a specific, clearly defined, measurable state. It's the difference between following a road that you know will get you to a certain destination and walking in the general direction of a destination you are not even sure about.

So how do you set goals that will get you to where you want to be? Well the first thing you have to do is to make sure that the clarity is there. If I were to ask you whether or not you have achieved a specific goal you must be able to give me an absolute yes or no answer.

Maybe or I don't know doesn't come into it. Either you have achieved your goal or you haven't, there is no in between. Are you a black belt or not? Can you kick to head height or not? Be as specific as possible when setting goals so you will know with absolute certainty if you have achieved them or not. That is the level of clarity you need in order to form a goal that your mind can lock onto and move towards rapidly.

Goals that are not written down are just fantasies in your mind. Always write your goals down to make them real and state them clearly for maximum clarification.

Goals must also be in writing in the form of positive, present-tense, personal affirmations. A goal that is not committed to writing is just a fantasy.

Set goals for what you want, not for what you don't want. Your subconscious mind can lock onto a clearly defined goal only if the goal is defined in positive terms. If you put your focus on what you don't want instead of what you do, you're likely to attract exactly what it is you're trying to avoid.

Phrase your goals as if they are already achieved. So instead of saying, "I will be a black belt next year" say "I am a black belt next year". Also be specific with times and dates and make sure each of your goals are measurable, so you would say, "I am a black belt by September 1st 2014". This provides you with a specific, measurable goal to work towards.

What if you want to set subjective goals, such as improving your speed or power or flexibility? To make such goals more measurable then you would use a rating scale of 1-10. So if your goal is to improve your speed then you would ask yourself, on a scale of 1-10, how do I rate my current level of speed? Then set a goal to achieve a certain specific rating by a certain date. This allows you to measure your progress and know with a high degree of certainty whether or not you've actually achieved your goal.

So that's long-term focus through goal setting and it will greatly enable you take control of your training and make sure it develops in the direction you want it to, as opposed to a direction someone else has set for you. Every training session should be about achieving those goals and putting your all into doing that. So let's now take a look at exactly how you can put your all into achieving your training goals.

How To Focus In The Moment

In training terms, if you can't give your full attention and concentration to whatever it is you are doing at any given moment then your progress will be inefficient and slow and you won't get to where you want to be in the time frame you have set for yourself.

So what's the best way to stay in the moment? Relax! Learning how to relax while your training is the single biggest thing you can do to aid your overall progress.

A lack of relaxation will lead inevitably to a rise in tension and thus a loss of concentration. You will no longer be in the moment and your mind will turn to distraction, fuelled by self-doubt and lots of little niggling worries over whether you are doing things right or not or should you be doing this or that instead and I don't deserve this belt and blah, blah, blah and on and on into a downward spiral of doubt and uncertainty that will absolutely effect your performance.

So the first thing you must do if you wish to stay relaxed as much as possible is meditate regularly, just like we discussed. Daily meditation will keep you focused and keep your stress levels under control enough so that the stress won't be creeping into your training.

Doing *Mokso* at the beginning of every session is also a great way to relax yourself and focus your mind towards the task at hand for it gives you the opportunity just to centre yourself and connect with the stillness within.

Never underestimate the power of breathing either when it comes to relaxing and focussing the mind. If you find your attention wondering then take a moment to do some deep breathing and you will find it much easier to concentrate afterwards.

Also keep reminding yourself why you are doing what you're doing. Remind yourself of your goals and the reason why you do martial arts in the first place. All of this helps you to focus your mind into the present and put all of your mental energy into your training.

Combining Focus

There is obviously a lot of information to take in here and you may be thinking that setting goals, discovering your overall martial purpose and trying to stay focused all the time is a lot to do, especially for something that you only do a few times a week.

Well, once you've actually worked out what it is you want from your training, setting goals to achieve that takes very little time and once you've done so it is only a matter of reviewing them occasionally to make sure you are staying on track and that you still want those things. After that it's just about maintaining focus in the way that we have discussed.

In the end, it boils down to this: you're going to put the time in anyway, so you might as well achieve something worthwhile while you're there. In five or ten years you are still going to be a martial artist (I assume) so wouldn't it be better to be the martial artist you *want* to be instead of the martial artist you *happen* to be?

Chapter 4: Neuro Linguistic Programming

"Human beings have a peculiar trait; if they find something they do doesn't work, they do it again!"

"Process is more important than content. If you alter the content, change takes for ever."—**Richard Bandler**

In the previous chapters we have looked at ways to calm the mind and free it from stress through meditation and also focus it in the right direction through visualization and goal setting. In this chapter we are going to look at a set of mind training techniques that together, make up the brain science known as Neuro Linguistic Programming (NLP).

NLP has been popular with people from all walks of life for many years now. Athletes especially have used it to enhance their performance in a number of ways, a couple of which we will be looking at here. Most of you will be familiar with NLP already, but for those of you that aren't, let's take a quick look at what NLP actually is and how it could help you become a better martial artist.

What is NLP?

Developed in the 1970s by John Grinder and Richard Bandler, NLP provides a way for you to get into yourself and understand how to be able to achieve success in a way many other motivated and well known individuals already have, including athletes, professionals from all walks of life and many martial artists.

These people went as far as they did because they knew they were able to do so. The creators of NLP realized that the things they were doing could be learned by others as well, and that if this were done effectively, anybody could do almost anything they set their minds to.

The name encompasses the three most influential components involved in producing human experience: neurology, language and programming. The neurological system regulates how our bodies function, language determines how we interface and communicate with other people and our programming determines the kinds of models of the world we create. Neuro- Linguistic Programming describes the fundamental dynamics between mind (neuro) and language (linguistic) and how their interplay affects our body and behaviour (programming).

Based on the dynamic interplay between these three fundamentals the creators of NLP have devised a number of techniques that make it possible for people using them to change their behaviour and the way they perceive themselves. In effect it is a form of brainwashing that you do to yourself for the benefit of making yourself better in some way, enhancing your performance as a human being.

 NLP puts itself across as a science –a science of the mind- though the established scientific community has never done anything to validate this claim and has in fact continued to refute its scientific credibility. There is no denying however, that NLP can have a positive effect on an individual who takes it seriously. Indeed many individuals and organisations across the world, including police forces, recognised athletes and many business communities will testify to the fact that NLP has really helped their overall performance, regardless of scientific validity.

I personally think NLP works because it focuses the mind so much. The techniques used force you to really examine your beliefs in a certain area and then put a lot of attention and focus on actually changing and making better that particular area. So really, NLP represents creative focus backed up by a willingness to improve. It's not really the techniques that matter as much as the time and energy you put into actually improving yourself.

So regardless of its scientific validity, NLP has been proven to work over the years, even if that's mostly on a subjective level. NLP is a subjective pursuit, but that doesn't make it any less valid here. I have used it over the years to improve many aspects of myself besides martial arts, so I know it works. The question is will it work for you? I obviously think it will, otherwise I wouldn't be writing this.

So let's crack on and look at two NLP techniques in particular that can help you improve your martial arts performance.

NLP Techniques

1. Modelling. Modelling is the main technique I want to discuss here because I think it holds the most use for us as martial artists. Modelling is a technique that was created to model the excellence of others. The basic idea was to be able to replicate the skills and abilities of experts. The modeller studies with precision every aspect of this expert. That includes his or her values, ethics, behaviour, habits, etc. The modeller then imitates the expert.

Now many NLP exponents tend to complicate this process by bringing in a lot of pseudo- scientific principles, to the point where the whole process becomes convoluted and almost unworkable for the average person. What I am going to do here is give you the method that I have used on a number of occasions with good success.

So the first thing you will do is select someone to model, which should be relatively easy if you're a martial artist. Most people choose their Sensei or instructor for obvious reasons. Your instructor will usually be very advanced and skilful compared to you and therefore will be the ideal person to model.

Once you have chosen the person you want to model, take yourself off to that quite room again and get yourself nice and comfortable like we talked about before with the meditation practice. Do some deep breathing and get your mind and body as relaxed as possible.

Now in your mind's eye begin to see the person you are modelling in action. If it's your instructor then picture them training, watch them perform their techniques in that very skilful manner of theirs. Examine how they move, how they breathe, how they position themselves, take in as much sensory information as possible. Do this for a few minutes or as long as it takes to get a good handle on their behaviour.

The next thing you are going to do is step into their shoes, so to speak. Actually feel yourself becoming that person and begin to feel how they move and react. Become that person in your mind, see things through their eyes and allow yourself to move in the way they do. How does it feel to be that person? How does it feel to move like they do? What do you think they are thinking? Allow your intuition to take hold here. This is a subjective process so there is no right or wrong way you should be feeling. Just go with the flow in your mind and be as vivid as possible in your imaginings.

When you start to get a real sense of this person your modelling step outside of them again and then picture yourself doing the same techniques but see everything in the first person and try to keep a hold of how it felt before when you were in that other persons shoes. Feel yourself move like they do, think of yourself as being on the same advanced level as they are. Do this for as long as you like or until you get a good sense of what it feels like to be at such an advanced level.

Doing this little exercise every day for a few weeks or so can have an amazingly positive effect on your martial arts performance. You will be quite surprised, as I was when I first tried this technique, at the results you get from it and you will notice a real difference in your technique.

You can take this technique even further if you wish by actually questioning your subject on the thought processes that go through their head when they are performing, processes that you can replicate in your own performance. The only problem with this is the very subjective nature of such processes and also the means used to illicit them in the first place, all of which makes accuracy of information quite difficult. The option is there though if you want to take things further.

2. Anchoring. Some sounds, pictures, smells, tastes or tactile sensations create special feelings in us. These sensations are called anchors in the field of NLP. A particular sensation which is connected to a person's particular behaviour, feeling, or thought is an anchor. The procedure in which an anchor is created is called anchoring.

Anchoring works on the subconscious level of the mind. Therefore, it is extremely powerful. You get anchored to various stimuli in the surrounding world. If a stimulus is anchored with a negative behaviour, it is a disadvantage. When you understand how anchoring works, you can break anchors which are of a disadvantage and create more useful anchors as you wish.

You see athletes using this technique all the time. When you see a tennis player make a fist and shout "Yes!" after scoring a point, that's anchoring. It's holding on to that positive, peak performance state, which is why it is especially useful for martial artists, especially those of you who compete in competitions.

If you need to be on top form at any given moment then all you have to do is activate your anchor and your body and mind will automatically go into the required state. How useful is that for sparring, gradings or competitions? Very, I'd say.

To make a successful anchor simply follow these instructions:

1. If your desired state is confidence, close your eyes, relax, sit erect, and relive a very powerful moment of your life when you were most confident, seeing what was there then in your mind's eye, hearing the sounds, feelings and other sensations. Your mind and body must be totally absorbed in the desired state.

2. Make the anchor when the state is at its peak. Make the anchor a special one. Make it an uncommon one such as pushing your right left finger backwards with your right hand, pressing your left wrist with your right hand or just clenching your fist and saying a word like "Yes!" in to yourself or out loud, it doesn't matter, as long as it's something quick, simple and easy to remember.

3. Keep repeating the anchor several times a day in the same manner for a few days until your desired state is firmly embedded to the anchor.

That's all you have to do. Now, when you need to be super confident for something, you just employ the anchor and your body and mind will go instantly into that state of confidence.

This is a very useful technique that I use all the time and you can anchor whatever state of being you like, whatever state you think will be useful to you in a given situation. Peak performance is generally what you are aiming for with this technique.

The two techniques we have looked at here are just two out of many in the area of NLP. I chose to concentrate on modelling and anchoring because I think they are the most useful for martial artists. If you are interested in learning more techniques then there is a wealth of books, videos and online information out there on the subject of NLP.

Like all such techniques you really have to commit to them and focus for you to get any real benefit from them. You also have to give them time to take hold in your mind and bring about any real changes.

Rest assured they do work, as I and many other people across the globe can testify to. They are just another way to focus the mind so we can better achieve our goals, both as people and as martial artists.

I don't think you can ever have too many tools in the box. It's just a question of which ones you like to use and which ones actually make your life easier. I believe the tools I have given you here do both.

Now it's time to take a look at the thing that often holds us back in training (and indeed in life) the most... fear.

Chapter 5: Fear And How To Manage It

"Fear is the mind killer."—**Ghandi**

"We are generally afraid to become that which we can glimpse in our most perfect moments, under the most perfect conditions, under conditions of greatest courage, we enjoy and even thrill to the god-like possibilities we see in ourselves at such peak moments, and yet, simultaneously, shiver with weakness, awe and fear before the same possibilities."—**Abraham Moslow**

Fear is a constant companion for most people, especially in today's urban environment where violence and confrontation are the norm. Out of all the emotions one can have, most people know fear the best, simply because it has such a powerful influence on us.

To have a life without fear in it is almost impossible for most people to imagine and indeed it is not really one you should try to imagine for fear is a constant of the human condition; it's as much a part of us as any other emotion and to try and rid yourself permanently off it is a fruitless endeavour.

That's the thing about fear—it never goes away!

But rather than let this fact get you down you should simply start to see fear as a necessary emotion and one which you should learn to utilize to your own advantage rather than let it impact you in a negative way. Fear is a powerful tool that will aid us in our response to confrontation and as martial artists we should make the effort to get to know it so we can better channel its energy into positive action.

That's what this chapter will aim to show you, how to turn an emotion that most people see as negative into something that is positive and useful to us as martial artists and people in general. Before we do that however, let us first get clear on what exactly fear is and the impact it can have on us.

What is Fear?

The dictionary definition of fear is:

"A feeling of distress, apprehension or alarm caused by impending danger, pain etc."

When the brain senses danger it triggers adrenalin which in turn triggers what is known as the fight or flight response, a massive dump of adrenaline that can be felt in the pit of the stomach and which urges us to react either way to the perceived danger- you either stay and confront it (fight) or you run away from it (flight).

The problem with this reaction is that it often causes terror immobilisation or the "freeze syndrome" in people. You literally end up rooted to the spot, unable to move or to make any clear decisions as to what to do next. This is why so many people view fear as a negative response, because of the debilitating effect it has on them.

The effect is only debilitating if you let it be, though. By releasing so much adrenaline from the adrenal gland into the system your body is actually trying to help you. For a short time your whole body will become turbo charged and ready for action. You will feel stronger, faster and your body will be partially anesthetised to pain, making you better able to handle a violent confrontation.

So if the fight or flight reaction is helpful to us in certain situations why do so many of us view it as being bad? The reason for that is because people have not trained themselves to react positively to the response and end up falling into a state of panic, caused when the reasoning process mistakes adrenalin for fear. This leaves a person drained of all that good energy and often frozen in fear in the face of the ensuing danger.

Adrenalin can also be released into the body in different ways, depending on the circumstances, the two most important of which for our purposes are slow release and immediate release.

A slow release of adrenalin occurs when you anticipate confrontation and the adrenaline can be released very slowly, sometimes over months, with the result that you end up feeling constant anxiety and what you perceive to be as fear over the anticipated event which can be an upcoming grading, for example, or a competition fight.

An immediate or fast release of adrenalin occurs when anticipation is not present or a situation escalates unexpectedly fast, causing an adrenal dump, as psychologists like to call it. The feeling is often so intense that a person will freeze in the face of confrontation because they mistake the feeling for sheer terror.

Within that there are also secondary occurrences of adrenalin that happen in a situation when things are not going to plan or you start to anticipate the consequences of a situation. Again, your body is just trying to help you along by doing this, not immobilise you with fear.

The sooner you start to recognize and acknowledge the adrenal response for what it is-- a means to help you- the sooner you can start to deal with your fear.

How to Confront Your Fears

The first step in the process of confronting your fears is self-honesty. You have to really look inside yourself and decide what your fears are and why you think you have them. Many people never get passed this initial first step because they are too often embarrassed or afraid to admit their supposed failings, maybe because they see it as weak to admit such things, which is ridiculous because we all have fears of some description. By admitting to them you are taking a major step in the right direction in conquering them.

As Geoff Thompson wrote in his excellent book, *Fear*, many people often say, "*It's not that I'm afraid, it's just that I don't want to do it.*" How many times have you said that to yourself and other people? I have used this excuse many times in my life and that's what it is, an excuse to avoid action.

Here's an excerpt from Geoff's book that eloquently illustrates this excuse syndrome very well and the extremely negative and debilitating effect it can have on you:

"As a younger person I would often convince myself that 'I'm not afraid of Karate competitions, I'm just not interested in competing'. If that was the case it would have been fine. In reality I found even the thought of competing nerve wracking and would experience slow re- lease adrenaline up to a couple of months before the contest. This long term anticipation would cause me sleepless nights and lessen my appetite. Lack of good food and sleep caused weight loss and depression. All of a sudden I was on a negative downward spiral, anticipation triggering many negative bodily reactions. The fact that I wasn't sleeping and eating would make me feel worse because, as I saw it, if I wasn't sleeping and eating then I must really have a problem. The lack of food and sleep would also make me very tired, being constantly tired lowered my defenses, leaving me at the mercy of the Voice, my inner opponent, who constantly told me how weak I was and how I couldn't handle it (the situation). Eventually I would get so down about the whole thing I would ring up my instructor and make up some silly excuse as to why I couldn't enter the competition."

So we have to be honest with ourselves if we are to overcome our fears and give ourselves the chance at reaching our full potential, as martial artists or otherwise. To do this we first have to make a list.

The Fear List

First take a piece of paper and write down whatever fears you think you may have. Remember, be honest with yourself. The whole world is not going to see your list, only you, so you have no reason to lie to yourself. If you have a fear of hitting or getting hit, then write those down. If your fear is competitions or facing off against someone with a knife, then write those down as well. Just be brutally honest, for that is the only way you can help yourself.

Now that you have your list of fears you now need to decide which one to work on first. It is advisable to choose the least of your fears first, the one you think will be easiest to conquer. Ordering your fears in this way means you can build on each success so that by the time you get to your biggest fear you have the confidence and will power to tackle it.

One way of ordering your fears is to do as Geoff Thompson suggests and create a "Fear Triangle", as he calls it. You put your smallest fear at the base of the triangle and then your next biggest fear after that and so on until you get to the tip of the triangle were your biggest fear will go. You then start at the bottom of the triangle and work your way up. This method allows for a steady progression and a gradual build-up of confidence over time.

The next step then is to tackle that fist fear.

Fear Exposure

In order to overcome any fear you have to be prepared to tackle it head on. There is no other way around this unfortunately. Facing your fears is something you can't hide from if you really want to conquer them.

So start with the smallest fear on your list, whatever that may be. As an example we will use a fear of public speaking, something many martial artists who are required to teach often have. The plan here is to expose yourself to the thing that makes you fearful, but to do so by degrees rather than just jumping in feet first.

If your fear is speaking in public then you would probably begin by speaking in front of just one person, perhaps teaching them a technique or explaining something to them. You would do this for as long as it takes for you to feel comfortable doing so. Once you feel comfortable enough talking to one person then you would move on to talking in front of two or maybe three or four people. The trick with this type of exposure training is to step just outside of your comfort zone but not so far that you end up freezing with fear again.

After a while you will start to feel comfortable speaking in front of a few people. Now it is time to increase that number to whatever you can think you can handle next. You will keep doing this over whatever time is necessary. You shouldn't push yourself too hard or you will end up losing confidence. Eventually, if you continue with this method you should be able to speak comfortably in front of many people, be it in the dojo or at a seminar or whatever.

Once you feel that public speaking is no longer a major issue for you then are ready to move on and tackle your next fear, thus working your way up the triangle until you get to the top where your biggest fear resides. Hopefully by the time you reach the top your confidence will have increased enough that you now have the bottle to deal with that fear.

And that's basically it, that's how you deal with fear. There is no secret to it or overly complicated process to follow. It's just a case of being honest with yourself and not allowing adrenaline to slowly poison you over time. If you really want to succeed in martial arts or your life in general then you must make an effort at over-coming the things that are holding you back from doing that with the methods described above. You must, to use a borrowed phrase, feel the fear and do it anyway.

Confronting your fears is probably the most beneficial and character building thing you can ever do for yourself. When you successfully face down your fears the world is your oyster and you realise you can achieve anything.

We have been conditioned, both by ourselves and by other people over the years to accept fear as something that is there to hold us back and stop us from doing the things we want to do, when in fact fear exists to help us do the things we want to do because it readies our bodies and minds for action.

This is especially true in the case of street self defense when we think we are feeling terror but it's just the process of our bodies becoming primed to deal with the situation. Bodyguards don't call the adrenal dump the "wow factor" for nothing. They know it's just the juice they need to carry them through a dangerous situation.

You should look at fear in the same way. Condition yourself to recognize the signs, to expect them and then to use them in the way that they are supposed to be used. Don't think of fear as fear, think of it as super-fuel that turbo-charges you into action. It's there for a reason and there isn't another substance on the planet that will so effectively help you in this way. Why should you be afraid when you have such powerful resources at your disposal?

And with that said, why don't we now journey to the dark side and get up close and personal with our sometimes greatest enemy of all...

Chapter 6: The Inner Opponent

"To think bad thoughts is really the easiest thing in the world. If you leave your mind to itself it will spiral you down into ever increasing unhappiness. To think good thoughts, however, requires effort. This is one of the things that training and discipline are about. So teach your mind to dwell on sweet perfumes, the touch of silk, tender raindrops against the shoji, the tranquillity of dawn, then at length you won't have to make such an effort and you will be of value to yourself."—**extract from James Clavelle's Shogun**

"The inner opponent is, basically, the voice or instinct that tries to warn you of the dangers that you face and the possible consequences of your actions. In general the inner opponent will advise you to run when danger rears its ugly head."—**from Dead or Alive by Geoff Thompson**

Without a doubt the biggest obstacle to our development as martial artists is not our ability to learn technique or our ability to win fights against others, but our ability to overcome ourselves, to tame and control the ever present opponent that lives within us all.

As if we don't have enough to contend with as martial artists we have this other person re- siding inside us whose sole aim, seemingly, is to try and hold us back by filling our minds with fear and doubt and insecurity, knocking our confidence at every turn and continually telling us that "*you shouldn't do that*", "*you'll never be able to cope with that*" and "*face it, you just don't have what it takes to succeed*". An overall helpful guy, I'm sure you'll agree.

With every challenge we face, the inner opponent is there, lurking in the shadows, testing our resolve at every turn.

But why? Why do we have this incessant voice of negativity inside of us all the time? Some would argue that it is there to help us, to keep us out of trouble and stop us walking into danger, which is true, to an extent. Just like fear, the inner voice is there to temper our behaviour but if you let it control you then all it does is hold you back.

One theory is that the inner opponent exists to make us stronger. If you can control and overcome a force as potent and persistent as that which lives within us then you can overcome anything.

If you can master your inner opponent then you can master anything, for no challenge is greater than that. Of course, by the same token, that makes mastering the inner opponent an extremely difficult task, but that's not to say it cannot be done. Anyone who has achieved greatness in their lives first had to master their inner opponent before achieving anything, but the fact is these people who achieved so much have succeed in that regard and therefore proved that it can be done.

Your inner self is the key to your success in any- thing, including martial arts. It is the rudder which steers you towards either success or failure. The layout of your inner self is reflected back at you in the layout of your life and is voiced by your inner opponent.

If your life is messed up it's because the way you are on the inside is messed up.

If you don't like the results you are getting from your training or anything else in your life then you have to change the nature of your inner self in order to get the results you want. Once again, it's about changing the internal reality to affect change in the external reality.

What you must remember about the inner opponent is that, al- though it is there to help us, it more often than not does just the opposite.

Learning how to control the inner opponent/critic, although a monumental task at times, is absolutely necessary to your success in any endeavour.

Getting results often means entering into challenging situations that will inevitably push us to our limits and for some people this is very hard to take and they end up backing away from such situations or running away altogether. But running away will get us nowhere, for we have to face and overcome these obstacles if we are to succeed in anything.

The reason many people end up backtracking is down to the fight or flight response we talked about in the last chapter. When we are really up against it our bodies tend to release adrenaline into our systems to help us out, either over time with slow release adrenaline, or right away with immediate release adrenaline. Unfortunately most people react to this adrenal dump the wrong way and end up channelling it into panic and fear, the result of which is that they freeze up or just run away.

We can't run away from everything however. Back in prehistoric times when the fight or flight response first originated, running away from things was probably a good tactic, because the challenges faced back then came in the form of Sabre-Toothed tigers and huge Grizzly bears. Hanging around to deal with such foes would have been folly, to say the least.

Unfortunately the fight or flight response has not evolved very well and remains the same as it was back in prehistoric times. Now, the challenges we face more likely come in the form of board room meetings and speaking in public, or as martial artists, rule bound competitive fights and gradings, situations that we shouldn't really be running away from but our initial response insists we do exactly that.

Added to this urge to run away from every challenge is the voice of our inner opponent who keeps pointing out the negative consequences in everything, making it harder for us to push on and see our challenges through.

That's why most people don't get nearly as much success in life as they should, because they don't understand their bodily reaction to stress and confrontation and they don't know how to handle the nagging voice of their inner opponent.

Having said all that you shouldn't feel bad for wanting to run away from situations. It's just natural instinct. If flight is an option then by all means take it. Problems only arise when flight isn't an option and you have to stand and face the music. In which case you really have to come up with a more proactive response to the situation. So just bare that in mind the next time you feel like a coward for wanting to run away.

So we've already talked about how to handle the adrenal response, so let's now look at how to deal with Mr Negative, our inner opponent.

As this is a book about mind training as it relates to martial arts we will assume here that we are talking about the inner opponent in the context of a physical or violent confrontation, but the techniques I'm about to put forth can just as easily be applied to any situation where you are feeling fear or an overwhelming urge to panic and run away, as in, to use a previous example, public speaking or a high profile meeting, or even your next grading or competition fight.

Thought Control

Thought control is the technique we are going to look at here, of which there are three variations, all of which involve you having a good degree of mindfulness, of being aware of your own thought processes.

Being mindful of how your mind works is half the battle when it comes to actually cutting out negativity. You have to be aware that the negative thoughts are there. Sometimes you cannot notice what is being thought in your own mind and you will therefore be influenced almost subliminally, without you even noticing. So be aware of what is happening in your own mind.

When your mind (or inner opponent) is bombarding you with negative thoughts then you have two options open to you. The first option is to simply ignore the negative thoughts, to not engage with them. By not engaging with negativity you will not be pulled in by it and will therefore be able to carry on regardless. However this is not as easy as it sounds as negative thoughts have an annoying habit of making themselves heard despite your best efforts, which is why we back this up with another tactic, which is Counter Thinking.

Counter thinking basically involves countering a negative thought with a positive one. Here's an example of that:

You're really scared

I am not scared, I'm completely fine

You can't handle this

Yes, I *can* handle this

You should run away now

No, I will *not* run away

By countering every negative thought with a positive one you are not giving the negativity a chance to take hold and influence your behaviour.

It is very important that you counter each individual thought because for every negative thought you let penetrate your psyche a small part of your will be eroded until eventually you will be facing defeat, both in your own mind and in the situation you are in. So it is very important that you keep those thoughts under control if you want to succeed.

The next technique we are going to look at involves blocking out the negative thoughts altogether by constantly repeating something positive in the form of a mantra or affirmation. This technique is very simple but very effective and prevents any negative thoughts from taking hold. So you would say to yourself:

I can deal with this, I can deal with this, I can deal with this, I can deal with this, I can deal with this...

Or:

I am in full control, I am in full control, I am in full control, I am in full control, I am in full control...

You get the idea. You can say anything you like to yourself just as long as it's positive and it empowers you and takes your mind of anything negative until you can do what you have to do.

Okay, so much for the techniques. Let's now try and draw some conclusions from all that info...

Conclusion

"Be master of mind rather mastered by mind."—**Zen Proverb**

For complete mind training to be effective you have to take a holistic approach to it which means you can't really view it as being separate from the rest of your training. Everything we have looked at in this guide, from meditation to visualization to focussing to NLP to fear control to managing your inner opponent, all of these techniques must be integrated into your existing training for them to be truly effective. As I said at the start of this guide, the techniques talked about here should only be used to supplement your physical training, not replace it.

The object of martial arts is to train the whole person, the mind, body and spirit together so that we develop in a balanced way. Train your inner self as much as your outer self but train both together. View yourself as a whole person and strive to develop yourself as such.

Really try to define what it is you want from life and the martial arts and then dedicate your- self totally to getting what it is you want.

Use whatever tools you have to get the results you want and if you don't have the tools then find them. You'd be surprised what resources you can find when you really have to. Always keep a good eye on your ultimate goal, for that will keep you moving in the right direction and ensure that you don't go off course.

All the techniques in this guide feed into one another. You will get the best results if you find a way to combine them all for the purpose of achieving whatever goals you have set for yourself.

If you truly desire what it is you want to achieve then nothing will stop you from doing that. Yes you will encounter many setbacks and problems along the way but if you use the tools you have at your disposal, like the ones I have given you here, and you continue to train hard and dedicate yourself then you will surely find success.

The greatest mental strength comes from training all the time, from dedicating yourself to the training 100% and constantly pushing yourself to the limit of your abilities.

By seeking discomfort you will be achieving true growth.

The more you put into it and the longer you stay at it the greater your mental strength will become.

Great mental strength comes from facing down your fears, overcoming your addictions and mastering yourself as much as possible.

This is what will allow you to handle pressure and overcome adversity and it is what will ultimately allow you to become great in life. You just have to want it.

Appendix A: How To Cultivate An Indomitable Warrior Spirit

It is often said in life that it is the journey that matters and not the end result. We learn more from being on the journey than we do when we actually complete it.

In martial arts training, it is also the journey that matters the most, not the rewards (the belts, trophies, certificates etc.) along the way. We obviously need the rewards because we have to have something to aim for, something to keep us moving along the path, things to help us continue on the journey and cultivate a warrior spirit.

Along this journey we will inevitably come across many obstacles that are put there to seemingly block our progress, pitfalls and hurdles with big stop signs in front of them that seem to signal the end of things.

In reality of course, these barriers to progress are not there to grind us to a halt, but to test us, to test our mettle to see if we are indeed worthy of continuing along the path we have chosen to travel on.

Many people, when they come across such obstacles, try to overcome them in a half-hearted manner, prodding the barrier a few times with a stick before deciding that they either don't have the inclination to attempt to find a way forward (and therefore use it as an excuse to quit the journey) or they simply feel they aren't strong enough to overcome the seemingly difficult or impossible odds.

This quitter mentality stems mainly from a lack of understanding as to the nature of the "journey" itself. The journey was never meant to be easy. It was never meant to be something a person could sail through unhindered. If it was we would all be on it and there would be no problems. However, there also wouldn't be any growth.

Personal growth and inner strength comes from confronting these obstacles and doing whatever it takes to overcome them. There will certainly be a lot of discomfort in your attempts to overcome them (the bigger the obstacle the greater the discomfort) but when you successfully do so, when you break down the wall in front of you to open up a whole new vista ahead, you gain a sense of enlightenment and personal growth. The bigger the obstacle you happen to overcome, the more personal growth and enlightenment you will gain.

Just understanding this fact alone can help greatly when it comes to breaking down those barriers. All it takes is persistence and a willingness to endure a certain level of discomfort and you will get there.

So given that, let's now take a look at some of the common obstacles and barriers to progress that we often come across as martial artists and see what the best way is to tackle them.

1. Injury. Martial artists, pursuing as they do a very physical pastime, often incur injuries of one kind or another. Most of these injuries are often not that serious, but despite this, they are sometimes enough to put people off from training any further.

It is not usually the injury in itself that stops people from training, but the excuse syndrome that comes with it. *"My knee is sore; I think I'll take a break from training for a while."* Or *"My ligaments are playing up, I need to rest."* These are normally excuses to back out just as the going gets tough.

The fact is, most injuries can be trained around. You hurt your hand, you use the other one. If your back is sore, don't do anything to aggravate it, do something else instead. Nine times out of ten, there will always be some kind of training that you can still do. I have a sore back most of the time, but it doesn't stop me from training. I know other people with crumbling knees and loose ligaments that still manage to train.

Obviously, if the injury is a serious one then it would be foolish to keep training if you are only going to make it worse. In that case, you should rest up. Even then though, you should still visit the dojo often and stay in contact with your fellow martial artists in order to maintain your interest and enthusiasm. Read; watch training videos, practice visualisation. Just don't cut yourself off from training altogether because you won't want to go back when you do finally heal.

Training through injury is a character building process and is excellent for developing a strong will and discipline to keep going through adversity (the warrior spirit), which is why you shouldn't make too big a deal of it when it happens. Just pick yourself up and carry on.

2. Boredom. This is one excuse that really annoys me when I hear it, mainly because it comes from a place of ignorance and a lack of understanding as to the nature of learning a skill.

When someone says, "*I'm bored with the training*," it means they haven't grasped the fact that in order to become anywhere near proficient in the martial arts you have to repeat the same techniques over and over again until they become second nature. That's how you get good.

The key to working past these issues is to change your perceptions of them. There are no shortcuts or other way around it.

If you look at any world class athlete, no matter what they do, be it shot putters, tennis players, swimmers, whatever, they are all good because they practice for several hours a day, doing the same movements over and over and over again until they have them as near perfect as they can get them.

This is what martial artists have to do as well; they have to drill the same techniques over and over in order to master them.

It's like the old adage says, to master any technique you must perform it at least 10,000 times (in a very deliberate manner of course, trying to make each rep better than the next). It doesn't matter what you're after—speed, power, strength, agility—you have to keep working at it. Yes, it's going to get boring, but that's the way it is.

Once again, working through the boredom is character building and growth stimulating.

3. Lack of Enjoyment. Similar to boredom in that people react to it in the same sort of way (i.e. they begin to question their commitment), a lack of enjoyment in training does not signal the end of the journey by any means.

You can't expect to do something like martial arts and enjoy it all the time. At some point, usually during a gruelling and painful training session your inner opponent will suddenly perk up and ask, "*Wait a minute, I thought this was supposed to be fun, I thought we should be enjoying this. This isn't enjoyable it's painful.*" At which point you will say to yourself, "*Maybe it's time I tried something else a bit more enjoyable…This isn't fun anymore.*"

Martial arts' training is a serious and at times gruelling pursuit, both physically and mentally, but that's the point. It's supposed to take you to your limits, to the point where you almost feel like quitting. However, the real enjoyment comes from seeing how much you have progressed after doing all those hard sessions, it comes from realising how much further on in your journey you have come.

It is unrealistic to expect to get enjoyment from it all the time. Many times in my training career I have lost that sense of enjoyment but I carried on regardless, pushing through the pain, so to speak. Lack of enjoyment is just another barrier to break down so we can become more enlightened. Stick with it and the enjoyment will return.

4. Lack of Progress. Every other week I bemoan my own perceived lack of progress. I say perceived because usually I am progressing and I just can't see it, though it often feels like I'm tracking through thick jungle, struggling in vain to find a way out, convinced there is none and that I am basically getting nowhere fast.

This happens to lots of people when they are training. They train diligently for weeks and months at a time thinking that they are getting nowhere when in fact they are progressing far more than they think.

The reason you think you're not progressing is because you are checking yourself constantly and when you do that you get blinded to your own progress. If someone actually watched you for one session and then checked back a couple of months later they would see a real improvement in you, simply because they haven't seen you for a while. It's possible to get too close to yourself, too caught up in yourself, to the point where you become blind to your own situation.

The fact of the matter is that with every session you do improve. How could you not? If you're not convinced then ask someone, ask your instructor and no doubt they will tell you the same thing. You just have to trust in the process, that's all. Stick with it and you will eventually get to where you want to be.

You should also understand that we improve the fastest as beginners. It's like bodybuilding—you make the most noticeable gains in the first few months. After that, although you still make gains, you make them over longer periods of time so they aren't as noticeable in the immediate sense.

Martial arts' training is exactly same. The longer you train the less noticeable your improvement becomes. Just remember though that although your improvement isn't as noticeable, it is still there nonetheless.

5. Responsibilities. The higher up the ranks you go the more responsibilities you tend to pick up along the way. As you get better you will be expected to teach other students, perhaps run classes and feel the pressure of having to maintain a high standard of technique in order to set a good example to those below you.

More than once I have resisted these responsibilities, resenting them for eating into my training time to the point where I was teaching more than training.

The black belt around my waist felt more like an albatross around my neck at times and like the Ancient Mariner, I thought about throwing myself into the sea more than once, so to speak. I considered quitting in other words. I was convinced my journey had come to an end without realising that I was just taking a new path to the same place.

I let my own selfish needs blind me to the fact that accepting and handling more responsibility is just another test along the way, yet another character building exercise and opportunity for further personal growth.

Once I faced up the challenge of actually teaching and looking after other people besides myself I was able to enjoy the sessions more because they were now a chance to grow and understand the techniques better (teaching is the best way to learn) rather than the dead-end I first saw them as being.

I also realised that if I wanted to maintain my own standards of technique then I would have to find other times to train, times when I could concentrate solely on my own advancement. I now do extra sessions when I can and train at home when I get a chance, just to stay on top of my own training.

Whenever you receive responsibility you shouldn't run away from it but instead see it as the opportunity for growth and experience that it is. Walking away from training altogether because things get a little bit more complicated is foolish and short-sighted. You owe it to your club and yourself to stick with the process and continue to grow and advance along the journey.

Change Your Perceptions

As I see it, those are the main barriers to progress that circumstance and our own perceptions of things often throw up to try and halt our progress. The key to working past these issues is to change your perceptions of them. Look at the bigger picture and see these tests for what they are--opportunities for growth and a chance to further develop that indomitable warrior spirit.

Appendix B: Self Discipline: The Bedrock Of Martial Arts Training

Self-discipline is something that I have struggled with quite a lot over the years and I'd wager that many of you reading this have struggled with it as well. As human beings we always have to push ourselves in order to do even the simplest tasks.

It seems we have a predilection for bouts of laziness were we refuse to do anything constructive with our time and choose to wile away the hours in front of TV or down the pub or smoking weed or whatever your favourite form of escapism happens to be.

The problem with this predilection towards laziness and ill-discipline is that it doesn't serve us very well in terms of achieving our goals and becoming who want to be.

If you are training in martial arts for instance, then in order to advance and get good you have to have the discipline to show up to class and actually train on a regular basis. Showing your face only once in a while is not going to get you anywhere.

I'm not going to pretend that I have some kind of formidable iron will that drives me to the dojo every single time I am due to be there because I don't possess such a thing. Most people I know don't possess such an iron will. I still miss the odd session, though admittedly this is usually through injury or good old fashioned tiredness through working hard at my day job. Sometimes I don't feel like I have the energy, even though if I probably pushed myself I'd be fine once I started training but I've already said I don't have the discipline of a Shaolin monk.

(Still, I have managed to keep training now for over thirty years, so that means I must have some discipline. I have also carved out a career as a writer so I'm not doing too badly.)

So in my quest for excellence I have looked in to improving my discipline and have come up with some methods to achieve this that have worked for me and which I am going to share with you now. You can thank me later when your instructor starts calling you by name instead of "*stranger*" or "*mate*".

Ways to Self Discipline

Way #1: Practice being disciplined. A few years ago I read a very popular article online by Steve Pavlina entitled, *How to be an Early Riser*. The article addressed an issue which a lot of people struggle with, which is dragging themselves out of bed in the mornings.

Now, I don't know about you, but I needed a crane to pull me out of bed most mornings. Rising from bed was for me like being forced to exit the womb all over again, complete with screaming match and lots of foot stomping around the house until I'd had my morning coffee.

When I read Pavlina's article I dove into it hoping to find a solution to a problem I'd basically learned to live with over the years.

Anyway, in the article, Pavlina advises that the only way to change the habit of hitting the snooze button fifty times is to actually practice getting up when the alarm goes off and to do so *immediately*. And how do you practice this? You get in and out of bed over and over again until the habit of rising the instant the alarm goes off becomes ingrained. I did this. For a few days I crawled in and out of bed for about an hour at a time until I was eventually able to rise in the mornings without too much difficulty.

If you are having problems getting yourself down the dojo then practice doing it. Pick a time, pack your stuff and walk out the door. Then go back in and do it all over again. Keep doing it until you don't even think about what you're doing. When you see it's time for practice you just go into autopilot and head out the door.

Such behaviour may seem laughable to you, but take my word for it (as someone who struggled to get out the door) it works. It's all about reconditioning your mind to react in a certain way once it's time for training. The key with this sort of discipline is just not to think about it. Go into autopilot and cruise on down the dojo.

Way #2: Create enough desire to motivate yourself. Desire is important when it comes to actually motivating yourself to train. If you find your discipline waning it is usually because your motivation is weak or no longer relevant to what you want to achieve in your training.

A strong motivation and well set goals that you really want to achieve will help greatly in spurring you into action, even at those times when you don't feel like doing anything except laying up on the couch.

If the lazy git inside you starts to talk you out of training then just think about why you are training in the first place and realise that you have to train to get what you want. Override the inner opponent with positive and motivating self-talk until you feel ready for action.

Successful people know they have to keep working on their goals every day, even if they don't feel like doing so, in fact, especially if they don't feel like doing so.

Way #3: Stay focussed. Staying focussed means setting goals and devoting your time to achieving those goals. A focussed mind is harder to dissuade than an unfocussed mind. An unfocussed mind is constantly open to influence from whatever sources of distraction happen to be around. I find it helps to actually write down on a piece of paper when I have to train and what goals I want to work on in a particular session. It's harder to argue with yourself when the task at hand is there in front of you in black and white.

Way #4: Work on developing yourself. I'm very into personal development and I find that constantly working on yourself to change negative behaviours and create more positive habits has an overall effect on your sense of self-discipline.

The more success you have in your life and the more things you do in your life, the more motivated you become and the easier it gets to be more disciplined with things.

I have found that success breeds success. There will always be things in our lives that feel like chores sometimes but these things are easier to get on with if you know that doing them will bring you success.

It's about trusting in the process of achievement.

Way #5: Move towards discomfort. A lack of discipline tends to leave a great big hole for a nice big comfort zone to develop. It's like moss on a stone, it only grows when we stand still, so we have to keep moving, and to keep moving we actively have to seek out discomfort and move towards it.

It is only in discomfort that we grow. There is no growth in remaining at home in your comfort zone when you should be experiencing a bit of discomfort down the gym or dojo. Discipline comes from not allowing yourself to sink into a comfort zone. Accepting discomfort into your life and realising that it is necessary for growth will by default make you more disciplined in yourself.

Learning To Bite The Bullet

The crux of the matter here is that you have to keep working at things all the time. Discipline, like most other qualities, does not come naturally or easily to most of us. We have to practice at developing it. Just as Socrates says in Peaceful Warrior, "*I practice everything.*"

Everything in life has to be practiced to some extent. In the case of discipline this means continually pushing yourself to do what you have to do, no matter if you feel like doing it or not. Moods, emotions, circumstances don't come into it. That's what marks out successful people from those who never achieve anything. Successful people know they have to keep working on their goals every day, even if they don't feel like doing so, in fact, especially if they don't feel like doing so.

I of course realise that this is easier said than done most of the time, but then nothing worth achieving is ever easy, is it? If it was we would all be raging successes in our lives.

So the next time you don't feel like training, block out the chatter from your inner-opponent and remind yourself of why you chose to train in the first place and then tell yourself that you'll never be any good unless you get of your ass and get out the door.

Accept the discomfort and just do it.

Appendix C: How To Really Commit To Martial Arts

A friend of mine got injured some time ago while training at the dojo. Not seriously, I'm glad to say, just a minor groin strain, but painful enough to keep him away from training. My friend, much like the rest of us, has had quite a few injuries of varying severity over the years but it seems this one in particular was just one too many. It was the proverbial straw that broke the camel's back.

My friend was so fed up he talked seriously about hanging up his *gi* and calling it a day, never to train in the martial arts again. I mean, here he was, in his mid-thirties and training in a highly demanding physical discipline more suited to someone half his age, allowing people to throw him around like a rag doll and put at times ridiculous pressure on his rather sensitive and over-yanked joints. If his sinews could talk they would probably scream for mercy.

"WHAT THE HELL ARE YOU DOING?" they would demand in a probably shrill voice. "YOU THINK THIS IS PLEASURABLE? YOU THINK THIS IS NORMAL, PUNISHING YOURSELF IN THIS WAY? NO MORE, FOR GOD'S SAKE…NO MORE."

And so for once my friend listened to his bruised and battered body. Maybe he wasn't being a sissy and over reacting after all, maybe partaking in such a gruelling pastime wasn't as beneficial to his health as he thought it was. Maybe martial arts' training was a hazard to one's health, a danger to its participants.

He began to wonder what the hell he got out of it at the end of the day. A set of hard won skills that he would probably never use for as long as he lived and if he did use them they probably wouldn't work as well as he thought they would. He would have spent years training for something that he would ultimately fail at. Where is the rational in that? Where's the sense?

A Crisis Of Confidence

I recall having a similar crisis of confidence many years back, shortly after I got my first black belt. My commitment failed me and I quit training with the vague notion that I had only quit temporarily, that one day I would return to training when I was ready.

I did return to training (thankfully). Seven years later. It was a long break, during which I was overcome by laziness, self-indulgence and a complete lack of discipline.

I never stopped thinking of myself as a martial artist but I was too stuck in my own indolence to actually do any training. I tried to return a couple of times but never lasted longer than a few months before my interest level fell drastically away and I just stopped training again, seduced by the comfort of my sofa and the insidious glare of my TV. Inwardly I felt ashamed for wasting myself in such a way. I felt dull inside, like I was on low grade sedatives all the time. I had little or no conscious awareness. If I wanted to use stronger words to describe the state I existed in most of the time during that period away from training, I'd say I was dead inside.

I can't put all these feelings down to just being away from the martial arts because that

would just be over emphasising the importance of one aspect of my life. The martial arts had played a big role in my life since the age of seven, but even so, other forces existed that were equally as strong in terms of influence.

I had little direction in my life back then and did little of any consequence to fill my time. As the saying goes, the devil makes work for idle hands. I exhibited behaviours that were not very beneficial to me, behaviours that had quite a negative effect on me and my life in general.

Your goals and motivations will change over time and you have to recognise this in your own mind so that you don't mistake a lack of motivation for a lack of commitment.

Luckily, I woke up eventually. At my lowest point I started to tap into my inner power again and I began to take heed of the wisdom that was inside of me. I got my act together. I reconnected with life and myself again and I have done my best to keep from looking back ever since.

Occasionally I can't help myself and I glance over my shoulder at the life I used to lead and I feel depressed at the thoughts of slipping back into it again, only this time, that would be it for good and I'd never be able to get back out again. I'd be stuck in a soulless life until the day I died. That vision is enough to keep me motivated to stay on the path I am now on.

A Purpose To Everything

I believe there is a purpose to everything that happens in this world, no matter how small or big that thing may be. Everything that happens in your life happens for a reason, even though you may not always be aware of that reason and it would seem to you that something is just random or serves no real purpose except to bring you misery. The dead years when I wasn't training in martial arts were a necessary thing in my life. They had to happen to get me where I currently I am. I needed to live those times in order to have the times I have now.

You may be wondering where I am going with all this? What does this have to do with my friend about to quit martial arts? Did he leave or not? Well, I'll tell you in a moment if my friend quit or not. What I am highlighting here is the importance of commitment in the martial arts and how difficult it is sometimes to maintain that commitment.

It is really difficult to keep training religiously week after week, year after year, like clockwork, doing the same sort of things over and over again with the amount of pain and discomfort you feel apparently increasing along with your skill level.

It's like you sacrifice something more to the art with every session, be it sweat, blood, tears or just inordinate amounts of pain. (Perhaps I'm exaggerating just a little. Perhaps the pain isn't that bad but you get used to it anyway, don't you? You realise this when newbies come along and they grimace at the tiniest of pressure exerted on them. You realise just how high your tolerance is and how much you can actually take. But I digress.)

Commitment ensures you keep going through the pain barrier and any other barriers that stand in the middle of your road to…what? Where are you going? Where do you want to end up? You need to know these things so you can decide if what you're doing is worth committing to. What are your reasons for training? Why do you keep at it?

When you know the answers to these questions you can then tap into the power of your resolve and use it to fuel the engines that keep you motoring along. When your commitment fails it means your motivation has failed. Rather than feel bad about how weak willed you are, take a close look at your motivations and find a way to fire up your desire again.

We have to keep re-inspiring ourselves through various means in order to really stick at something. Initial desires and motivations often wane over time and they lose their power to spur you into action. They need re-evaluating.

You need to be really clear on why you keep turning up at the dojo however many times a week. When you're completely clear in this way then it's just a matter of employing a bit of self-discipline to keep you active.

All the self-discipline in the world will not spur you into action if deep down, you really don't want to do it. You really have to want to train in martial arts in order to do it. That may sound obvious, but I suspect a lot of people kid themselves for whatever reason into thinking it is something they do want when in fact they would much rather do something else completely. An honest evaluation of your motives is needed for real commitment to take hold.

If you're motivated enough then you will find it easy to commit to training. If you find it hard to commit, change your motivation, and if that doesn't work then maybe you should spend your time doing something else. It's that simple.

And by the way, my friend went back to training. Despite the period of doubt he suffered his motivation was strong enough in the end to keep him committed. His resolve to keep training was even greater than before, as mine was when I decided to recommit.

Renew Your Commitment

No one ever said it was going to be easy. You will always have ups and downs throughout your training career, times when you will feel like giving up altogether. At such times the only thing that will keep you going is your resolve and your commitment to your goals.

Your goals and motivations will change over time as well and you have to recognise this in your own mind so that you don't mistake a lack of motivation for a lack of commitment.

If you're pulling away from training then it's because the reasons you had for training before are not resonating with you anymore, not because you are not committed to the training itself. Rediscover your reasons for training and your commitment will come back again.

Training in martial arts is a journey you take and like all journeys there will be inevitable complications and times when you will feel stuck and you will feel like you're not progressing at all. You need these challenges in order to grow however.

Sometimes you fail but each time you fail success will become ever closer. Overcome the challenges and you will be all the more powerful for doing so.

Appendix D: The Value Of Persistence

You ever wonder why the drop-out rate amongst martial arts students is so high? Is it because the training is hard? Is it because it is repetitive and at times hard to enjoy? Is it because students realise that they really want to be doing something else? Or do they quit when their dreams of being like Bruce Lee after three months training don't materialise?

The Value Of Persistence

Most likely all of these things play a part in the high drop-out rate but in my opinion, the reason that most people quit is because they lack persistence. They fail to see that success can be theirs if they just stick at it but often times, their perceived lack of progress and absence of faith in the learning process and the ways of the universe make it all too easy for them to become pessimistic about what they are doing and their once strong resolve caves in under the pressure of all that negativity and of course they quit.

To succeed in anything you have to be persistent and tell yourself that you are not going to give up until you do succeed. It is essential to have the right mindset or else your inner opponent will systematically destroy any hope you have of ever reaching your goal by filling your mind with negative thoughts and emotions.

Once these destructive thought patterns take hold it is very difficult to see past them and sooner rather than later they will fulfil their promise of making you quit something that you once optimistically thought you would succeed in.

Many student drop-outs would have succeeded if they had just hung in there a little longer. If they had realised that success was closer than they initially thought they would maybe have persisted a little longer and got to where they once so badly wanted to be.

The Tipping Point

I'm sure you have heard of "the tipping point". The tipping point is a phrase created by Malcolm Gladwell in his book of same name.

Tipping points are "the levels at which the momentum for change becomes unstoppable." One never knows when one is going to reach this point, it could happen anytime, so it is best to keep going, knowing that the tipping point will happen eventually, it's just a matter of time.

All other factors discounted, sheer persistence will usually get you to where you want to be. It's how most martial artists make it to black belt level or master a kata or get good enough to win a competition. They just put the time in.

Consider this example. A person could practice a technique ninety-nine times and still not get it right so they decide to quit trying and they walk away having failed in their quest to master that technique.

However, unknown to that person, they had reached the tipping point, that fine line dividing success and failure and if they had just practiced that technique one more time they would have gotten it right. Just one more time was all it would have took. But that person would never know this because they had quit too soon.

It is also essential to realise that the ninety-nine times you did do the technique are what brought you to success in the first place. The tipping point couldn't have occurred without first practicing all those times beforehand and what made you practice all those times beforehand was persistence.

So we never know when the tipping point is going to be but we know it is going to be at some point, so it makes sense to carry on in good faith, knowing that success will happen eventually.

Looking Down The Mountain

Not to get too clichéd here, but success is very much like climbing a mountain. I've never climbed Everest but I imagine the climb would be tough going and many times during the assent I would feel like giving up before I got to the top.

At this point it would be beneficial to ignore the advice to not look down and to turn your head and take a good long look at just how far you've come in your journey. We quite often get so caught up in striving towards our goals that we miss just how much progress we have already made.

We quite often get so caught up in striving towards our goals that we miss just how much progress we have already made.

So if you're training towards some goal in the martial arts and you're thinking that you are never going to get there, it really helps to pause and look back over your journey so far. I think you'd be surprised at how much progress you've actually made. Give yourself some credit for getting as far as you have. Doing so really helps to motivate you into carrying on.

Don't Give Up Your Dreams

Don't give up on trying to achieve your goals. I recognise that it is sometimes a great strain to carry on in the face of seemingly insurmountable odds but these obstacles are character building and give you the inner strength to handle the success when you get it.

So the next time you feel like you are not making any progress in your training, or indeed in the achievement of any goal that you have set for yourself, take the time to look back and to see how much you have achieved already.

Sometimes this retrospective look over your shoulder can be enough to rekindle your motivation. If it isn't then remember the tipping point. Success could just be around the corner. Tomorrow or the next day or the day after that could be the day that everything falls into place and you get the breakthrough that you need to propel you into success.

Appendix E: Battling Negativity

I was speaking with a friend once when he mentioned he was suffering from acute anxiety attacks. He explained that he was getting slow release adrenaline constantly and that he felt like he was in fight mode all the time.

The only respite he got from this condition was when he was training. Shortly after the session though, the anxiety would creep back up on him again and his mind would begin to work overtime, whipping up a maelstrom of negative thoughts and using them to feed the feelings of panic and anxiety my friend was feeling in his body.

It appeared to him that his body and mind were working against him instead of for him.

I could sympathise with my friends condition because I once suffered from the same sort of thing (as I'm sure many others have): perpetual worrying about the future; being controlled by negative thought processes; and lacking in confidence and self-esteem because of it.

It can feel like you are trapped inside your own mind sometimes and that the world is conspiring against you.

All in all, not a very positive or pleasant way to live your life, being at the mercy of unfounded fears and constant anxiety about a future that never happens.

It's debilitating and stops you from making any real headway in your life.

Too often we talk about protecting ourselves from others who wish us harm. Rarely if ever do we talk about protecting ourselves from ourselves.

I'm talking about self defence against the self.

Your negative self, the darker side of your personality, is a foe you are more likely to face than some mugger on a street corner or some mouth-piece in the pub who wants to take you outside and make hamburger meat out of your ass (however that sounds!).

I find it strange that many martial artists go to great lengths to learn how to deal with violence outside of themselves, but forget, or neglect to learn how to handle the violence that is continually doing them damage on the inside.

Negativity in our thoughts and behaviour, expressed every day of our lives, sometimes without us even realising it, is more damaging to us than any number of punches landed on us by some thug.

Negativity is no less violent in its intent, and its intent is to destroy us from the inside out, but only if we let it.

Would it not make more sense if we spent more time learning how to become more positive individuals in our thoughts and actions; spent more time learning how to control our own minds instead of allowing our minds to control us?

If most of us put the same amount of effort into developing ourselves as people as we do fighters, we would be far better off, I believe.

It's a mammoth task, taking control of your own mind, and one which I struggle with most of the time. I think many people underestimate the effort it takes to first gain control off, and then stay in control off, your mind. You have to be on guard 24/7, which can often prove to be impossible, not to mention exhausting.

Years ago I made the decision to try and take control of my own destiny. Since then I have learned to control my own mind (to some degree at least). Most of my thinking is positive now and I try to stay in the moment as much as possible, so I don't end up worrying about the future. Consequently I don't suffer from anxiety much anymore. The thoughts that once caused that have been banished or kept under control.

But where does one start defending the self against the self?

My friend asked me this as well. I advised him to cultivate his self-awareness and become conscious of his own thought processes. That he had to be an observer inside his own head, observing without judgement what was going on in there, what kind of thoughts were floating around and what effect those thoughts had on his feelings and behaviour.

You can't defend yourself against something that you don't know anything about. You wouldn't train techniques without first knowing about the type of threat those techniques were meant for. Know thy enemy and all that.

I also told my friend that he had to try and put a stop to his negative thought processes by either countering them with more positive thoughts or by just letting them pass him by without engaging with them too much- just letting them pass like clouds in the sky.

That was the biggest thing for me, learning to be aware of your thoughts so you can control them better.

My friend said he got respite when he was training. This is because in training, you are in the moment, thinking of nothing else but of what you are supposed to be doing.

Moving without thinking.

Focus can be the key to staying in the moment, as we have already seen. When we train, we are completely focused on what we are doing. There is no room for negative thinking.

The lesson here is that you should have some sort of purpose in your life, something to aim for and work towards so that you don't end up directionless and overly susceptible to boredom and idleness.

Having a well thought out life purpose can work wonders for a person. It keeps you focused and less prone to negative thoughts and behaviours. If you are working towards something you simply don't have time to be negative or think about the future too much.

Another key lesson in combating negativity is to accept that doubts, fears and uncertainties will always be present within your mind.

No matter how focused you are you will always still wonder if you are really on the right path, or doing the right thing in the right way. Dwell on this too much and your progress will grind to a halt. You will never do anything because you are not sure about anything. You end up paralyzed. Just accepting these feelings as normal will allow you to move forward despite them. You have to have faith that things will happen as they are meant too.

Everyone's approach to it will be different. You have to find your own path to inner-peace. It doesn't matter what kind of path you take, as long as you hold the intention in your mind of wanting more self-control so you can fulfill your potential as a human being.

Bear in mind: No one is positive all the time.

Everyone has bad times, where everything seems to go wrong.

Expecting to be positive all the time, being hard on yourself because you aren't, will just make things worse.

It is better to adopt a policy of self-acceptance.

Think to yourself: *Okay, so I'm down at the moment, whatever, it can't last forever*.

And it won't.

Sometimes it is better to accept your feelings than to fight them.

About The Author

Rory Christensen has been a practicing martial artist for over thirty years now. He is a 5th degree black belt in Goju Ryu and a 2nd degree black belt in Shotokan karate. He has also trained in various other arts, including Kenpo, Jujitsu, Aikido and Kali. He resides in California with his wife and three daughters.

Made in the USA
Lexington, KY
19 March 2019